We're Off… to Peru

Nos Vamos… a Peru

By Georgette Baker

We're Off… to Peru/Nos Vamos… a Peru
Copyright 2010 all rights reserved
Published by Cantemos
Chino Hills,CA
Telephone 800-393-1336

No portion of this book may be copied or reproduced in any form without the written consent of the publisher.

Photographs by Michael Mastorakis and Linda and Greg Umberg
Special thanks to the Umberg family for the use of their photographs.

Peru is the third-largest country in South America
and is approximately three times the size of California.

**Perú es el tercer país más grande de Sudamérica
y es aproximadamente tres veces el tamaño de California.**

Peru does not have an exclusively tropical climate. The climatic varies within the country: arid and mild in coastal areas,

Perú no tiene un clima exclusivamente tropical. El clima varía dentro del país, árido y templado en la costa,

temperate to frigid in the Andes,

templado a frío en los Andes,

and warm and humid in the jungle.

y tibio y húmedo en la selva.

One of the most famous ruins in the world is in Peru. It is called Machu Picchu and was built by the Incas.

Una de las ruinas más famosas del mundo está en Perú. Se llama Machu Picchu y fué construido por los Incas.

In the Quechua language
Machu Picchu means 'Old Peak'.

En el idioma Quechua
Machu Picchu significa "Pico Viejo".

The cloud covered ruins have palaces, baths, temples, storage rooms and many houses,

Las ruinas anubladas incluyen palacios, baños, templos, cuartos de almacenamiento y muchas casas,

carved from the gray granite.

tallados de granito **gris.**

Most of the native people of Peru, are of Amerindian origin.

La mayor parte de las personas nativas de Perú, son de origen amerindio.

The two main endemic races that inhabit Peru are the Quechua and the Aymara people.

Las dos razas dominantes que habitan en Perú son los Quechua y los Aymara.

The highest navigable lake in the world is in Peru and part of Bolivia. It is called Lake Titicaca. It is in the Andes Mountains at an altitude of around 12,500 feet.

El lago navegable más alto del mundo está en Perú y parte de Bolivia. Se llama Lago Titicaca. Está en las montañas Andinas a una altura de alrededor de 12.500 pies.

In Lake Titicaca there are 45 islands. The Uros Islands are in the National Park 40 minutes by boat from the city of Puno, Peru. The base of the islands are made of reeds and clay.

En Lago Titicaca hay 45 islas. Las Islas Uros están en el Parque Nacional 40 minutos por barco de la ciudad de Puno, Perú. La base de las islas está hecha de caña y barro.

The Uros peoples, the inhabitants of the islands, use bundles of dried totora reeds to make reed boats and to make the islands themselves. Each island takes 1 year to build and lasts 25 to 30 years.

Los Uros, los habitantes de las islas, utilizan cañas secas para hacer los barcos de caña y para hacer las islas mismas. Cada isla toma 1 año para construir y duran de 25 a 30 años.

Another wonderful part of Peru is the Amazon Rainforest and the Amazon River. The Amazon River of South America is the largest river in the world and has a series of major river systems in Peru. 2/3 of Peru is covered by the Amazon Rainforest.

Otra parte maravillosa de Perú es el Río Amazonas y la selva Amazónica. El Río Amazonas de Sudamérica es el río más grande del mundo y tiene una serie de sistemas de ríos en Perú. 2/3 de Perú está cubierto por la selva Amazónica.

There are many bugs, snakes and mosquitoes in the jungle. At night it is best to sleep in a hammock and covered by a mosquito net.

Hay muchos insectos, serpientes y mosquitos en la selva. De noche es mejor dormir en una hamaca y cubierto por un mosquitero.

There are piranhas and caimans in the river.
This little caiman we caught and let go.

Hay pirañas y caimanes en el río.

Este caimán chiquito lo agaramos y lo soltamos.

Peru is also a diverse country, with modern buildings and cities too.

Perú también es un país diverso, con edificios y ciudades modernas.

It is also a country with beautiful handmade items.

También es un país de bellas artesanías.

I can't decide what I want as a souvenir, the sweater or the hat..

No se que llevarme de recuerdo, el sueter o el sombrero…

GLOSSARY

Exclusively: use by a single individual or group

Granite: a very hard natural igneous rock

Inhabitants: one that occupies a particular place regularly

Piranhas: Types of fish, some species are meat eaters

Temperate: not extreme

Ruins: remains of one or more destroyed buildings

Exclusivamente: uso por un solo individuo o grupo

Granito: una roca magmática muy dura

Habitantes: uno que ocupa regularmente un lugar en particular

Pirañas: tipo de pez, algunas especies son carnívoros

Templado: no extremo

Ruinas: restos de uno ó mas edificios destruidos

Michael Mastorakis, who you see in the photographs, was the original author of "We're Off to the Galapagos". He has been keeping diaries since he was four years old. As of now, 2010, Michael is studying engineering at the University of California San Diego and continues to travel, take photos and keep journals.

Look for his first adventure

"We're Off… to the Galapagos/ Nos Vamos…a Galápagos"

and

"We're Off… to Kenya/Nos Vamos …a Kenya"

"We're Off… to Australia's Great Barrier Reef/

Nos Vamos a la Gran Barrera de Australia "

We're Off…to Australia's
Great Barrier Reef

$12.95 bilingual book

We're Off…to the Galapagos
/Nos Vamos…a Galapagos
$12.95

We're Off…to Kenya
Nos Vamos…a Kenya
$12.95

www.simplespanishsongs.com 800-3931336 or amazon.com, Baker and Taylor Books or Follet Library Resources

Funemic Awareness
of the Spanish Language

CD and book with piano music and text. Enhance phonemic awareness with fun renditions of La Bamba, La Cucaracha, Guantanamera, Chocolate, The Chicken Dance, Una Mosca.   **$12.95**

Settle Down Sounds
Ten, three minute relaxation exercises for the classroom. Teach students how to refocus, relax, increase memory, creativity and awareness.

$9.95 each

Sonidos Serenos
Bilingual CD of relaxation exercises. 5 Spanish and 5 English, with: classical music, Tibetan chimes, wind sounds.

Multi-Ethnic Stories
CD and book in Spanish and English

Indian tale *The Blind Men and the Elephant*, **Native American** *story about the origin of man*, **Chinese** *Zodiac, The Origin of the* **African** *tale about justice* and **Mexican** *story/song "the origin of chocolate"*.
PLUS A LISTENING GAME **$10.95**

CUENTOS Y CANCIONES The Little Red Hen, ABC's, Days of the Week, Las Mananitas, Vengan a Ver Mi Granja, La Sombra , stor y of Periquito, Un Elefante, everything in English and Spanish
Guitar chords included. **$12.95 CD/Book ages 3-10**

AESOPS FABLES / LAS FABULAS DE ESOPO CD with 6 Stories in English and Spanish CD **$10.00**

CANTEMOS CHIQUITOS A collection of 14 of the most popular Latin American Classic children's songs, in Spanish and English with accompanying bilingual songbook, some piano music. LOS POLLITOS, TENGO UNA MUNECA, QUE LLUEVA, DE COLORES, PERIQUITO, CON REAL Y MEDIO, ARRURRU, EL SAPITO, EL GUSANITO. **CD/BOOK $10**

CANTEMOS CHIQUITOS # 2 More Songs from South the Border 20 songs and fingerplays in English and Spanish. Includes LA CUCARACHA, 5 LITTLE MONKEYS, plus VOWELS, COLORS, NUMBERS AND 6 holiday favorites (Noche de Paz, Jingle Bells, Cantemos, Noche Buena, Gloria).Full orchestration, bilingual song book with piano music included. **$10.95 CD and Book**

Canciones Patrioticas Americanas/Patriotic Songs $10

www.simplespanishsongs.com 800-3931336 or amazon.com, Baker and Taylor Books or Follet Library Resources

www.ingramcontent.com/pod-product-compliance
Lightning Source LLC
Chambersburg PA
CBHW081357040426
42451CB00017B/3483